The English Seaman and His Remarkable Wife

By

Bonnie S. Johnston

THE ENGLISH SEAMAN AND HIS REMARKABLE WIFE

BY BONNIE S. JOHNSTON
COPYRIGHT 2016

This is a narration of information about two early families who contributed much to the settlement of America. The information is compiled from first hand sources, census records and court documents, and second hand sources, family stories and historical documents. The material is not designed as a source for proof of genealogical information, but rather to encourage additional research. The author has combined historical information with family stories and logical conclusions in describing the moves and adventures of these early settlers.

Book design by author.

Author contact: bonniesnotes@yahoo.com

Narratives by Bonnie S. Johnston

The Germans
The Road from Jamestown
Early New England Settlers

Historical Novels by Bonnie S. Johnston

The Dark Side of the Mountain
The Dark Side of the Trail
The Dark Side of the River
Tales of the Frontier

The English Seaman and His Remarkable Wife

The emigrant Richard Stout and his famous, remarkable wife Penelope provide fascinating early American history and are the progenitors of the majority of present day Stouts. Their marriage and lives provide the plot for an historical novel as well as insight into early American history. Many generations later several of their descendants made the move from New Jersey to the newly settled lands of Ohio where descendants remain to this day. This family fought in the early Indian wars, lost several members in the American Revolution, and provided men for all of the wars in which America has become engaged.

The American branch of the English Stouts descends from one John Stout of Nottinghamshire, England. His line is clearly documented and descends from his son

Richard who settled in New Amsterdam, New York, by 1642. Many records exist, and Richard's descendants can easily document their heritage to him. Recent research suggests that the English Stouts were descended from Norsemen who came to England during early raids of the Vikings. At that time the name was "Stoudt". Olaf Stoudt was the Earl of Orkney and Shetland in the eleventh century and was a member of the royal family of Norway according to one legend. In 1220 a Stout was a leader of the Danes who fought the Irish and was killed in the process. In any event, the Stouts existed several centuries in England before Richard Stout came to America around 1642. The name Stout, both the English and German derivatives, comes from the word "stout" to describe the physical characteristic of stoutness.

John Stout

One John Stout of "good family" was recorded in the Burton Joyce parish register of Nottingham, England, as marrying Elizabeth Bee on November 13, 1609. This couple had at least one child recorded as Richard, born as early as 1610 but usually stated as 1615. Family tradition records that Richard fell in love with a woman below his standing. She may have been a servant in Sir John's household. After a bitter quarrel with his father who did not approve of the match, Richard joined or was pressed into, the British Navy for seven years. He may have simply run away from home. He was approximately twenty years old at the time of his enlistment. The female with whom Richard fell in love is unknown to history.

Traditional stories record that after the seven years, Richard was discharged and chose to leave his ship at New Amsterdam, America, about 1641 or 1642 when he was twenty-six or twenty-seven years old. There is no proof of Stout's service and there are alternative theories, It is highly unlikely that a British naval ship would have been allowed to enter the New Amsterdam harbor since the Dutch were at war with the British at that time. It is much more likely that Stout left his ship in New England, if indeed, he were discharged from the British navy.

It is possible that Stout came to New England with Lady Deborah Moody who established herself and her followers near Salem for religious purposes. The group were Antibaptists. There is a record in Lynn,

Massacheuttes, suggesting Stout came with Moody. If so, he was not discharged from a navy ship at all. It is also possible that he did leave the British navy and simply joined Lady Moody and her followers when he arrived in New England. Perhaps he disagreed with his father over religion rather than a woman and simply decided to join Moody in England before she sailed to America.

Regardless of the reasons that placed Stout in New Amsterdam, he was there in 1643 when he was listed as fighting for the Dutch against the Native Americans. Moody had received a grant from the Dutch to settle the new village of Gravesend at the southern tip of Long Island. She and her followers had found New England much too restrictive in religious practices, intolerant toward Antibaptist views. The group then fled to Rhode Island, then to New Amsterdam for aid from the Dutch.

Stout became a landowner in Gravesend and a prominent citizen. Traditional accounts never suggest that he was married before he was forty when he finally married the fascinating Penelope. It is highly unlikely that he had not been married, however, and it may have been that he had a wife and perhaps one child when he first resided in Gravesend. It is very probable that his wife died, leaving him with at least one son. Since he embraced the Antibaptist faith with Moody and her followers, records of births do not exist and the dates of the births of his children are inclusive at best.

When the English took over New Amsterdam in 1664, Richard was readily accepted since he had fought for the Dutch as their subject. He was said to have been "a man of parts but of little formal education" according to a descendant who recorded the Stout family history in the early 1800s. Since he signed his will with an "x", he could not write; descendants refute his lack of writing ability and attribute it to "infirmity" of old age. It would seem many ancestors possessed this infirmity. However, since Stout was of "good family", it is likely that he had received some education in England and most likely could read and write.

Penelope Van Princin (Kent or Prince)

In 1647 or 1648 Richard Stout married Penelope Van Princin, Prince, or Kent. She was a woman of courage and the subject of many stories and early histories. One traditional view suggests that, in 1622, Penelope was born in Amsterdam, or as some say, Sheffield, England, a daughter of Reverend Kent, a Baptist preacher from Sheffield, England, who had been driven out of England for his religious views. By 1643, Penelope had married a Dutchman called Jan Van Princin, and the couple headed for America the same year.

Tragedy struck this Dutch ship on a point of land called Sandy Hook, New Jersey. The ship crashed against the rocks and sank. Some of the passengers and crew made it to shore, but only the crew lived to travel to New Amsterdam. However, the young Van Princins were left on the shore, the husband being injured and feverish.

Hostile Indians soon attacked, killing Van Princin and injuring Penelope whom they left for dead. She suffered a severe concussion, fractured arm, and a gash allowing her intestines to protrude. Finding refuge in a hollow tree, she no doubt expected death at any moment and languished in this terrifying condition for a few days existing on berries. One story states that an old Indian stopped her from execution believing she would die anyway. He later returned to get her.

It seems highly unlikely that the crew of the *Kath* would leave a young couple alone and make their way to New Amsterdam, over forty miles by land. They would have known of the Indian danger and the fact that it would be many days before a search party could return to the desolate shore of New Jersey. They would have known that a young Dutch couple could not survive alone since the husband was wounded. Furthermore, they could have constructed a litter to carry the young man with them since Penelope was not injured until after the crew left.

Another version relates that two Indians on a hunting expedition came close to Penelope's hiding place, and she either called to them, no longer fearing death, or they discovered her hiding place. The younger Indian wanted to kill her but the older, a chief, won out and carried her to their village near the present site of Middletown, New Jersey. He cared for her wounds which he sewed with a fish bone needle and vegetable fiber thread. She eventually recovered and remained as a squaw for perhaps one year.

According to researcher Linda Stout Deak, the Dutch ship *Kath*, owned by Hans

Jelisz of the West India Company, left Amsterdam in June 1647 for Sandy Hook, New Jersey. November 1648 entry records show the ship did not return. Five ships from Holland sailed to the new world between 1639 and 1648. It is unlikely two sank on Sandy Hook, a place where some say two thousand ships have sunk over many years. The *Kath* is very likely the ship upon which Jan and Penelope Van Princin sailed if this story is true.

Another account recognizes the *Kath* but reports that the ship arrived at New Amsterdam before June 9, 1647. It was then ordered to cruise against the Spaniards. It was reported in Curaco in February of 1648. In July it captured a Spanish bark and brought it north to Manhattan. In a suit on July 2, 1648, the captain and crew requested pearls taken from the Spanish ship in payment because the *Kath* had been stranded on Sandy Hook and they wanted final wages. Therefore, Penelope, if she were aboard, did not reach America until late 1648, and had been aboard during the trip to Curaco. There was no mention of a ship wreck or stranded passengers in this Gravesend record.

According to other stories, when the news of a white woman's capture finally reached New Amsterdam, men went to the village to ransom Penelope. It is assumed that the Indians had indicated that they had a white captive. The Indian chief who had rescued Penelope asked what she wished to do. Replying she wished to go to New Amsterdam, the chief accepted the payment offered, and Penelope went to live with English families in Gravesend rather than Dutch families in New Amsterdam. This fact suggests that Penelope was not Dutch but rather English. The year, originally thought to be 1642, was more likely 1648 if this tale is true. She later met Richard Stout and they were married. A copy of their marriage entry exists in the Hopewell, New Jersey Museum but the date is not clear. Penelope would have been about twenty-six years old.

Penelope's remarkable exploits have been recorded in several early sources. A descendant reported that she wore a headdress to cover her scalp wound; she also had little movement of her arm plus the scars on her abdomen. She reportedly told her grandson who questioned her Indian wounds, *"Johnny, put your hand in the pocket of my garment and feel the scares of my wounds, then you will know it is true and you can tell your grandchildren it is true, and they can tell their grandchildren it is true..."*

Some researchers insist this remarkable woman lived to be 110 years old and had 502 descendants in 1732. However, others maintain that she died in 1712 at age ninety, perhaps a more realistic date during that time. She was most likely buried on the family plantation in Middletown, New Jersey. Her youngest child was born in 1669 when she was forty-seven years old.

Recent information has poked holes in this remarkable account of Penelope. It is most likely her last name was Prince. She was not the widow of someone named Kent or Van Princen. Rather she was Penelope Prince, indentured servant of Kent Island. This information is recorded in the estate papers of William Cox, resident of Kent Island. It is now presumed that she ran away from her indenture, joined other dissidents, and eventually made her way to New Amsterdam where she may have concocted the traditional story to maintain respectibility among the settlers. Perhaps the last name of Kent evolved from the fact that she was from Kent Island.

That she had been involved in an Indian attack is probably true but the circumstances might be very different from the story passed down. She and her companions may have been attacked on their way to Gravesend at some point causing her scaring mentioned in several family histories.

It is also probable that Stout assisted her in her story that she had been shipwrecked and widowed, left to survive on her own, later with the help of the Indians. It is also possible that Stout already had one or two sons and needed a wife. Penelope is listed as Penelope Prince in a court record of Gravesend in 1648 incidating she was still single and the marriage to Stout could not have been before that date as many have previously stated. Stout's oldest sons' birthdates suggest they might have been born before then. Since there are no official birth records for the Antibaptists, we may never know the truth. Many granddaughters were named Penelope, suggesting the naming patterns of the time; however, even if she were stepmother to one or two of Stout's sons, they no doubt considered her their mother since they would have been very young at their birth mother's death.

One record of Stout's land purchase in 1664 mentions a son "of age" that year. "Of age" indicates that this son was at least 18 years old putting his date of birth 1645 or 1646, before Richard and Penelope married in 1448. This record strongly suggests that Stout had at least one son perhaps by a first wife.

Richard Stout

At age twenty-eight, Richard Stout, after his seven years service, perhaps as a British privateer or sailor, took up residence in the fort at New Amsterdam, according to traditional accounts. That same year, 1643, Stout was employed by the Director General Wilhen Keift, to aid the fort during the Indian uprising in February. It is proven that Stout was in New Amsterdam by 1643 but it remains unproven exactly when he arrived or if, indeed, he left a Naval ship.

In the meantime Lady Deborah Moody, an Anabaptist wealthy widow, requested and was granted, permission from the Dutch to lay out Gravesend, now a part of Brooklyn. The town Gravesend was allowed religious freedom.

Lady Moody was quite a woman for her time and certainly was the first woman to lay out and manage a town. She had come to New England in 1639 and had been excommunicated by the Anglican Church. She died in 1659 in Gravesend where memorials to her still exist.

Byh 1643 Stout no longer practiced the Anglican religion but embraced the Antibaptist faith and was a lifelong Baptist, and it is very likely he came with Moody or joined her in New England.

An interesting record in New Amsterdam October 1643 states that Richard Stout was deposed for stealing pumpkins and hogs. Stout and others accused members of the crew of *Sevenster* and *LaGarce*, British privateers, appeared also. It is not clear if Stout was a crewmember or a conspirator or even if they were guilty. But the record does connect Stout to New Amsterdam and Gravesend.

In December of 1645, thirty-nine patentees existed for the newly laid out town of Gravesend. In February 1646, Stout received Lot #16. He grew tobacco and sold his crop for 210 guilders. In 1645, Stout had received Lot #14 at the first division of Gravesend, Long Island, now a part of Brooklyn. In 1646, he received Lot #11 at the second division of Gravesend. Richard Stout was over forty years old and Penelope twenty- two when they married in 1647 or 1648.   By 1657 their "plantation" numbered thirty four acres in Gravesend.

In 1661 Stout bought Lot 26 in Gravesend. In 1663 Stout brought suit against Nathaniel Butler who accused him of selling wine to Indians. Stout won the suit and Butler paid the costs. In 1666 Stout sold seven acres in Gravesend.   In 1664 the Dutch had surrendered New Amsterdam to the English and New York came into existence. That same year 12 men from Gravesend signed the Monmouth Patent for land in New Jersey, Stout was one. The cost of this land was 118 fathoms seaswamp or wampum, five coats, one gun, one clout cap, one shield, 12 #s tobacco and one tanker of wine. It is difficult to comprehend the prices paid for land in the new world at that time. Only four of the patentees moved to New Jersey, the Stouts being one. The colony of New Jersey allowed religious freedom and the Stouts were Baptists. They became founders of the First Baptist Church of New Jersey.

Having purchased what is now in the county of Monmouth, New Jersey, Richard bought Lot 36 plus, in all, 745 additional acres. By 1678 Richard had accumulated over 1800 acres and was considered the largest landed proprietor in New Jersey. It is interesting that the Stouts chose to settle the area of Penelope's captivity with the Indians, if indeed, she had been captured and held in the New Jersey village.

The couple's first child was thought to be born in 1645. However the *Kath* did not sink until at least 1647. There is also a record of September 12, 1648, where Penelope Prince was involved in a case of slander and accused a woman of milking a neighbor's cow. The woman was acquitted and Penelope states she was sorry for the accusation. This record as well as the history of the *Kath* suggests Penelope did not arrive in New Amsterdam before 1647 and was still single in 1648. Therefore, their first child must have been born in Gravesend around 1648 or 9. Their children's birthdates have never been confirmed, but several accounts suggest that children were born before 1649 indicating there is the possibility of Stout having a first wife who had died before then. This possibility is rarely discussed since Stout descendants claim descent from Penelope rather than a first wife, understandable considering Penelope's prestige among famous women. Furthermore, so far no indication of a first wife has been found.

Another story of this couple's adventures is as follows, according to traditional accounts. After the founding of Middleton, New Jersey, the old chief who had saved Penelope appeared at their home in New Jersey. He refused the offer of goods and proceeded to tell Penelope to flee in his canoe with her children for the Indians planned a midnight attack. When she informed her husband, Richard refused to believe his wife, but she gathered her children and paddled toward New Amsterdam for help. After she fled, Richard reconsidered, gathered the men of the area together and sent their families to safety. At midnight the Indians did indeed attack, but the settlers were superior with their guns and called the Indians to parley and settled the dispute. A two day meeting occurred, and a Treaty of Peace ensued. The whites agreed to purchase the land and an alliance was faithfully upheld. The date of this purchase or patent was January 25, 1664, the Monmouth Patent signed by Richard Stout and twelve others. At that time there were fifty white families and five hundred Indians in the area were Middletown, New Jersey, was founded.

This story probably relates to an incident in Gravesend, not New Jersey. Penelope could not have paddled across the bay to New Amsterdam from New Jersey, the distance being too great for a canoe; however, she could have done so from Gravesend when the Indians attacked the community because only a river separated the two places. There were no Indian attacks on Middletown, New Jersey, in the 1660s, but there were several attacks on Gravesend. The story has been passed down for hundreds of years as the story of Penelope has been embellished and distorted.

Richard and Penelope were very active on their new "plantation" in New Jersey where documentation exists. In 1668, the settlers met in the Stout home to form the first Baptist Church in New Jersey. In 1669, Richard was one of the overseers for Middletown. In 1670 Penelope with her ten children went with Richard to New York, formerly New Amsterdam, where an entry records a purchase of a new "slavy", indicating the Stouts were slave holders and prosperous.

In 1674, Richard and his children received "rights of Land", 780 total acres. In 1679 Richard received a patent for 460 acres. In 1678 Richard served on a jury at Middletown when a man was charged with taking a whale off the New Jersey coast for his own use. In 1690 Richard and Penelope conveyed to son Benjamin the plantation they lived on at the Hop River, New Jersey, after their decease. From 1676 to 1684 Stout dispersed land to his several sons.

In June 1703, the will of Richard Stout was filed in Trenton, New Jersey, and proven October 23, 1705. Richard's will was signed with an X suggesting he could not write. However, many researchers believe that he must have had some education due to his father's standing in England. At the time of writing his will, he may have been ill or incapacitated in some way. He was ninety years old at the time of his death. His ten children included John, Richard, James, the birth dates uncertain, Mary born 1650, Alice born 1652, Peter born 1654, Sarah born 1656, Jonathon born 1660, David born 1667 in Monmouth County New Jersey, and Benjamin born 1669 also in Monmouth.   Both Stouts lived to be very old for their times.

The will of Richard Stout
(Recorded in Liber I, p 120, of Wills at Trenton, New Jersey)

Know all men, by these presents that I, Richard Stout of Middletown, in the county of Monmouth, in East Jersey, being of Sound Mind and disposing memory, do make and ordain this to be my last will and testament which is a followeth;

I will that all my just debts be paid; I give and devise unto my loving wife, during her natural life, all my orchard and that part of rooms of the house she now lives in, with the cellar, and all the land I now possess. I give and bequeath unto my loving wife, all my horse kind, excepting one mare and colt. My son Benjamin is to have for keeping my cattle last year.

I give unto my sons John, Richard, James, Jonathan, David, and Benjamin, one shilling each of them.

I give unto my daughters, Mary, Alice, and Sarah, each of them one shilling.

I give to my daughter-in-law Mary Stout and her son John one shilling each of them.

I give and bequeath unto my kinswoman May Stout, the daughter of formerly Peter Stout, one cow, to be paid within six days after my wife's death.

All the remainder of my personal estate whatsoever, I give and bequeath unto my loving wife and to this, my last will and testament, I make my son John and my son Jonathan my executors to.

For this my will performed, in witness hereof I have hereunto put my hand and sear, June the ninth day, in the year one thousand seven hundred and three.

His

Richard X Stout

His Mark

Signed, sealed and unpublished in the presence of us: Richard Hartshorne, John Weekham, Peter Vandervere

Proved before Lord Cornbury, Governor, Captain General, and Etc. 23 October 1705 at Perth Amboy.

David Stout

David Stout, the seventh son of Richard and Penelope, was born in 1669 in Middletown, New Jersey, where the family moved from

Gravesend. He married Rebecca, daughter of James Ashton and Deliverance Throckmorton, who had resided on Manhattan Island very early.

Rebecca was born in 1672 in Providence, Rhode Island, and died in 1725 at fifty-three in Amwell. The couple married in 1688 in Hopewell, New Jersey, where other members of the Stout family had settled. David died in 1732 in Amwell, Hunterdon County, New Jersey, where he had moved earlier. He was fifty-six years old. David and Rebecca had five sons and three daughters and lived the majority of their lives in Middletown. The children who survived were James, Freegift, David, Joseph, Benjamin, Rebecca, and Sarah. David lived several years longer than his oldest son James who died in Amwell in his thirties. These Stouts are buried in Stout-Manners Family Cemetery near Wertsville on land given by David Stout.

James Stout

James Stout, born in 1695, was the eldest son of David and Rebecca Ashton Stout. In 1712, at the improbable age of seventeen it is thought, he married Catherine Simpson, who was several years older; the couple had seven children, six sons and one daughter. The family had moved to Amwell, New Jersey, and purchased 700 acres. But at the age of thirty-six in 1725, James contracted pleurisy and died suddenly leaving a widow with seven children. His father David had moved to Amwell before and provided the burial ground for the Stout family. Catherine Simpson Stout must have been a remarkable woman. She married a second time Samuel Stout, a cousin of her dead husband's. Samuel was only four years older than her oldest son and quite a few years younger than the widow. The marriage proved successful and produced one son, Samuel, who is well recorded in records.

Joseph Stout

Joseph Stout, son of James and Catherine Stout, was born in 1717 in Amwell, New Jersey. He was only eight years old when his father died suddenly. But he soon found himself with a stepfather, his father's first cousin Samuel Stout. Evidently Samuel provided the appropriate influence because records suggest a harmonious family.

Joseph married Mary Hixon in Amwell, New Jersey. Joseph died in 1760 at age forty three. A Joseph Stout fought in the Revolutionary War; however the Daughters of the American Revolution believe that this Joseph was not the husband of Mary or the father of Benijah but rather a relative.

Benijah Stout

Benijah Stout was born in 1740 in Amwell, New Jersey, on his father's farm. He married Elizabeth Hyde in 1760 in Amwell, the daughter of John Hyde born in 1705 perhaps in England. The couple had nine children. Their eighth child was Charles who was born in 1783. For some reason, Benijah, his wife Elizabeth, some of their children and other members of the Stout family decided to settle on the newly offered Ohio land near Cincinnati. James Denham of New Jersey was a land speculator and offered land for sale around the turn of the century. Benijah was sixty-one when he left his native New Jersey to make an arduous journey. The family probably went overland to Ft. Pitt by wagon, then by flat boat to Cincinnati, Ohio. The family settled in what is now Colerain Township, Hamilton County, Ohio. In 1810 the Hamilton County Tax List included Benijah, sons Charles and Ruben, and James and Jesse Stout, relatives. Benijah died in 1823 at age eighty three and was buried on his farm in Colerain Township. Elizabeth died October 1, 1821, and is buried in Colerain Township, probably on family farm.

Charles Stout

In 1801, Charles was eighteen years old when his parents moved to the newly opened settlement of Ohio. He was born in March 16, 1783, in New Jersey and died January 14, 1866, in Colerain. He was eighty-three at the time of his death. At age twenty-six he married Mary Duvall in 1809 in Butler County, who was born March 3, 1790, in Virginia or Kentucky. The couple were Baptists and had twelve children. Stout Road in Colerain is named for the family. She died January 10, 1859 having lived sixty-nine years. One theory is that Mary's father may have been Benjamin Duvall of Virginia, and her brother Benjamin, born 1791, in Virginia, and a resident of Colerain. They are buried in the Old Baptist Cemetery in Bevistown, Ohio.

Duvall

Mary Duvall, wife of Charles, is thought to have been born in 1790 in Virginia or Kentucky. Mary and Charles were married in Butler County in 1809. She no doubt came to Colerain with her parents since a nineteen year old female would not have moved alone at that time. The Duvalls must have been in Ohio before 1809. Another theory of Mary's ancestry is a connection to Mathew Duvall, a resident of Colerain Township and born in Mongahela County, Virginia, a son of Marsh and Rebecca Duvall. Mary was probably related to this family. She may have been a sister of Matthew Duvall. She may also have been the daughter of Benjamin Duvall and sister of Benjamin born in 1791 in Virginia. Both groups died in Colerain Township and were probably related.

Benjamin Stout

Benjamin Stout, son of Charles and Mary Stout, was born in Colerain on the family homestead. He married in 1850, Elizabeth Ann Hill, born in 1832. The couple had one hundred acres near Bevistown. They had nine children including William, Frank, Edward, George W. plus daughters.

Anna E. Hill was an orphan whose guardian was Aaron R. Sayre. She was born in 1832 and at the time of her marriage in 1850, she was seventeen years old. Her guardian, Sayre, signed for her. One of Aaron and wife Charlotte Sayre's sons married a Stout so the families were well connected in the Colerain area. Her parents were born in New Jersey according to the 1850 census. William Hill was Anna's father, according to Anna's death certificate. No information has been found regarding him; however, he was probably from New Jersey and came with others to settled Ohio, where his wife died and he left at least one daughter, Anna Elizabeth. The Sayre's were early Ohio settlers and may have also come from New Jersey.

George Washington Stout

George Washington Stout was born November 6, 1859, on his father's farm. He married Cora Moore of Amelia, Ohio, and worked for the Estate Stove Company in Mt. Healthy, Ohio for forty years. The Stouts had three children, and the author descends from their daughter Helen who married Glen Marcum.

George's early memory is of sitting on a fence on his father's farm in Colerain Township, Hamilton County, Ohio, where he and his father Benjamin watched Morgan's raiders ride through the county during the Civil War.

Cora Moore, George's wife, was the daughter of William Moore and Elizabeth Gardner, both of who came from families who settled Clermont County early in the 1800s. The Gardners descended from Nathan Gardner, Revolutionary War veteran and the early Salem settler Thomas Gardner. William Moore descended from early Irish settlers who moved from Virginia to Ohio before statehood. William's father Enoch Moore settled in Adams County, Ohio, around 1800, but his father has not been documented.

There are tens of thousands of Stout desendants today in almost every state. Most of these Stouts descend from the remarkable Penelope and Richard Stout. Regardless of whether one believes the flawed historical accounts, Penelope was certainly a remarkable woman as was her husband. Both were pragmatic and resourceful. If they concocted the stories of Penelope's shipwreck as well as the Indian connections, they were extremely clever. If Penelope were a runaway indentured servant, historical tales provide her with four hundred years of fame for hiding it. She deserves our respect regardless of her origins.

It is impossible here to list the Stout descendants and those of prominence throughout history. For further research, the internet and family histories can provide information about Richard and Penelope's descendants.